W9-BGK-681

BLEEDING, BLISTERING, AND PURGING
Health and Medicine in the 1800s

DAILY LIFE IN AMERICA IN THE 1800s

BLEEDING, BLISTERING, AND PURGING
Health and Medicine in the 1800s

by

Matthew Strange

Mason Crest Publishers

MASON CREST PUBLISHERS INC.
370 Reed Road
Broomall, Pennsylvania 19008
(866)MCP-BOOK (toll free)
www.masoncrest.com

First Printing
9 8 7 6 5 4 3 2 1

Library of Congress Cataloging-in-Publication Data

Strange, Matthew.
 Bleeding, blistering, and purging : health and medicine in the 1800s / by Matthew Strange.
     p. cm. — (Daily life in America in the 1800s)
 Includes bibliographical references and index.
 ISBN 978-1-4222-1775-7 (hardcover)   ISBN (series) 978-1-4222-1774-0
 ISBN 978-1-4222-1848-8 (pbk.)   ISBN (pbk series) 978-1-4222-1847-1
 1. Medicine—United States—History—19th century—Juvenile literature. I. Title.
 R151.S85 2011
 610.97309'034_dc22
                         2010025295

Produced by Harding House Publishing Service, Inc.
www.hardinghousepages.com
Interior Design by MK Bassett-Harvey.
Cover design by Torque Advertising + Design.
Printed in USA by Bang Printing.

Contents

Introduction

History can too often seem a parade of distant figures whose lives have no connection to our own. It need not be this way, for if we explore the history of the games people play, the food they eat, the ways they transport themselves, how they worship and go to war—activities common to all generations—we close the gap between past and present. Since the 1960s, historians have learned vast amounts about daily life in earlier periods. This superb series brings us the fruits of that research, thereby making meaningful the lives of those who have gone before.

The authors' vivid, fascinating descriptions invite young readers to journey into a past that is simultaneously strange and familiar. The 1800s were different, but, because they experienced the beginnings of the same baffling modernity were are still dealing with today, they are also similar. This was the moment when millennia of agrarian existence gave way to a new urban, industrial era. Many of the things we take for granted, such as speed of transportation and communication, bewildered those who were the first to behold the steam train and the telegraph. Young readers will be interested to learn that growing up then was no less confusing and difficult then than it is now, that people were no more in agreement on matters of religion, marriage, and family then than they are now.

We are still working through the problems of modernity, such as environmental degradation, that people in the nineteenth century experienced for the first time. Because they met the challenges with admirable ingenuity, we can learn much from them. They left behind a treasure trove of alternative living arrangements, cultures, entertainments, technologies, even diets that are even more relevant today. Students cannot help but be intrigued, not just by the technological ingenuity of those times, but by the courage of people who forged new frontiers, experimented with ideas and social arrangements. They will be surprised by the degree to which young people were engaged in the great events of the time, and how women joined men in the great adventures of the day.

When history is viewed, as it is here, from the bottom up, it becomes clear just how much modern America owes to the genius of ordinary people, to the labor of slaves and immigrants, to women as well as men, to both young people and adults. Focused on home and family life, books in this series provide insight into how much of history is made within the intimate spaces of private life rather than in the remote precincts of public power. The 1800s were the era of the self-made man and women, but also of the self-made communities. The past offers us a plethora of heroes and heroines together with examples of extraordinary collective action from the Underground Railway to the creation of the American trade union movement. There is scarcely an immigrant or ethic organization in America today that does not trace its origins to the nineteenth century.

This series is exceptionally well illustrated. Students will be fascinated by the images of both rural and urban life; and they will be able to find people their own age in these marvelous depictions of play as well as work. History is best when it engages our imagination, draws us out of our own time into another era, allowing us to return to the present with new perspectives on ourselves. My first engagement with the history of daily life came in sixth grade when my teacher, Mrs. Polster, had us do special projects on the history of the nearby Erie Canal. For the first time, history became real to me. It has remained my passion and my compass ever since.

The value of this series is that it opens up a dialogue with a past that is by no means dead and gone but lives on in every dimension of our daily lives. When history texts focus exclusively on political events, they invariably produce a sense of distance. This series creates the opposite effect by encouraging students to see themselves in the flow of history. In revealing the degree to which people in the past made their own history, students are encouraged to imagine themselves as being history-makers in their own right. The realization that history is not something apart from ourselves, a parade that passes us by, but rather an ongoing pageant in which we are all participants, is both exhilarating and liberating, one that connects our present not just with the past but also to a future we are responsible for shaping.

—Dr. John Gillis, Rutgers University
Professor of History Emeritus

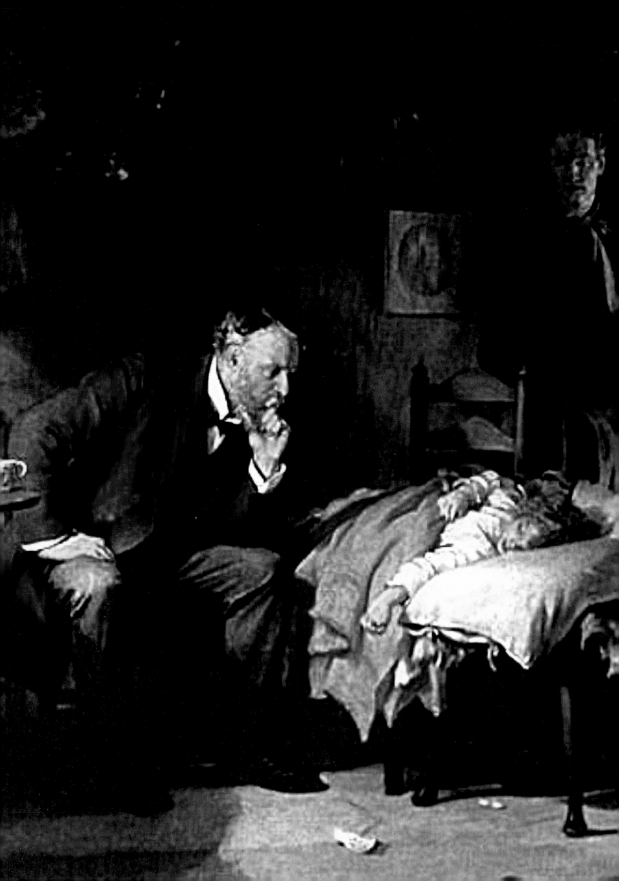

Part I
Where Were the
Doctors?
(1800–1832)

1800

1800 The Library of Congress is established.

1800 Humphry Davy discovers the anesthetic properties of nitrous oxide.

1801

1801 Thomas Jefferson is elected as the third President of the United States.

1803

1803 Louisiana Purchase—The United States purchases land from France and begins westward exploration.

Time Line

1816

1816 Stethoscope is invented—French physician René Laënnec invents the stethoscope, learning how to correlate the various sounds he hears to diseases of the chest.

1818

1818 First successful blood transfusion—performed by Dr. James Blundell, an obstetrician.

1820

1820 Missouri Compromise—Agreement passes between pro-slavery and abolitionist groups. It states that all the Louisiana Purchase territory north of the southern boundary of Missouri (except for Missouri) will be free states, and the territory south of that line will be slave.

1804

1804 Journey of Lewis and Clark—Lewis and Clark lead a team of explorers westward to the Columbia River in Oregon

1812

1812 War of 1812—Fought between the United States and the United Kingdom

of the 1800s

1823

1823 Monroe Doctrine—States that any efforts made by Europe to colonize or interfere with land owned by the United States will be viewed as aggression and require military intervention.

1825

1825 The Erie Canal is completed—This allows direct transportation between the Great Lakes and the Atlantic Ocean.

1832

1832 Cholera epidemic leaves 3,515 dead in New York City—the equivalent death toll in today's New York City would be over 100,000.

NOTICE.
PREVENTIVES OF
CHOLERA!
Published by order of the Sanitary Committee, under the sanction of the Medical Counsel.

BE TEMPERATE IN EATING & DRINKING!
Avoid Raw Vegetables and Unripe Fruit l.
Abstain from COLD WATER, when heated, and above all from *Ardent Spirits*, and if habit have rendered them indispensable, take much less than usual.

Being sick is awful. There is nothing much worse than that moment you know for sure that it's not just your allergies acting up, or a passing sniffle. The only thing that some people might consider worse than the sickness itself is the trip to the doctor that soon follows. But if you think about what Americans in the past faced instead of the competent medical care we receive today, you may find yourself feeling grateful for our medical professionals.

With diseases like AIDS making headlines in our modern world, you may feel as though we still face a world of germs against which we have no protection. And to a certain extent, that's true. But people in the 1800s had it far worse!

Just as the transition into the nineteenth century occurred, Americans were facing an epidemic like nothing they'd ever seen before—yellow fever. Caused by the bite of certain mosquitoes, the deadly virus turned skin yellow and attacked the liver and kidneys. About half of all the people who got sick with yellow fever ended up dying. Although it was mostly focused in seaport cities and never made it far inland, in 1793 alone, it killed one out of every ten people living in Philadelphia. Until the 1820s, it returned often to attack Northern cities like New York and Baltimore, while in some Southern cities, like New Orleans, yellow fever returned annually until after the Civil War.

Tiny mosquitoes spread a disease that killed thousands of Americans.

EXTRA! EXTRA!

Memphis News
The Fever Time in Memphis

Yellow fever arrived in Memphis by steamer and quickly spread from the docks to the rest of the city. The authorities then went at their work, but it was too late, except to cleanse and disinfect the city. The deaths grew daily more numerous; funerals blocked the way; the stampede began. Tens of thousands of people fled; other thousands, not daring to sleep in the plague-smitten town, left Memphis nightly, to return in the day. From September until November hardly ten thousand people slept in town over night. The streets were almost deserted save by the funeral trains. Heroism of the noblest kind was freely shown. Catholic and Protestant clergymen and physicians ran untold risks, and men and women freely laid down their lives in the service of others. Twenty-five hundred persons died in the period between August and November. The thriving city had become a charnel house. But one day there came a frost, and though too severely smitten to be wild in their rejoicings, the people knew that the plague itself was doomed. They assembled and adopted an effective sanitary code, appointed a fine board of health, and cleansed the town. Memphis to-day is in far less danger than Vicksburg or New Orleans or half a dozen other Southern cities, of a repetition of the dreadful scenes of last year.

This terrible visitation did not prevent Memphis from holding her annual carnival, and repeating, in the streets so lately filled with funerals, the gorgeous pageants of the mysterious Memphis—such as the Egyptians gazed on two thousand years before Christ was born—the pretty theaters being filled with the glitter of costumes and the echoes of delicious music. The carnival is now so firmly rooted in the affections of the citizens of Memphis that nothing can unsettle it.

America was still a young country, and younger still were its cities, where diseases like yellow fever spread quickly and then lingered. Some people worried that these epidemics might make urban living impossible. These fears seemed to be validated when, not long after the last of the waves of yel-

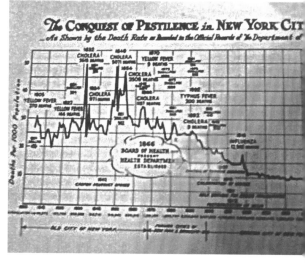

This chart shows the death rates caused by cholera and yellow fever in New York City during the 1800s.

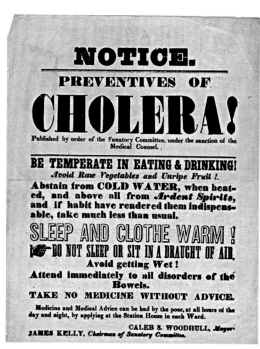

No one understood the causes of cholera, and so the public was advised to stay warm and dry as a preventative measure. Avoiding raw vegetables and fruit, however, may have helped to prevent the disease being passed along on these foods.

low fever hit Northern cities, another epidemic took root: Asiatic cholera.

By the end of June 1832, cholera had found its way to New York City by way of Canada, and it would reach Philadelphia and Cincinnati by mid-July, Boston and Baltimore by August, and then travel south to New Orleans by October. Almost no urban area along the East Coast of the United States was spared cholera's wrath. Some Americans saw the epidemic as a sign from God that people in cities were not living the way they should be, and that the community was being punished.

EXTRA! EXTRA!

Editorial, 1832
Western Sunday School Messenger

Drunkards and filthy, wicked people of all descriptions, are swept away in heaps, as if the Holy God could no longer bear their wickedness, just as we sweep away a mass of filth when it has become so corrupt that we cannot bear it. . . . The cholera is not caused by intemperance and filth, in themselves, but it is a scourge, a rod in the hand of God.

Cholera was not God's punishment for sin (no more than AIDS today is a punishment for sin!). Instead, cholera was actually a bacterial infection of the intestines. It caused massive diarrhea and dehydration, and it could take a person's life in a matter of hours. At the height of the epidemic in New York City, 2,500 people died in about two months. The city's economy was brought to its knees, and its citizens were terrified. But nowhere was hit as hard as New Orleans, where the loss of life (relative to population) was three times as bad as it was in Northern cities like New York.

Unfortunately, the technology of transportation was far ahead of medical knowledge, and the disease easily followed major travel routes between the nation's urban areas. The rural communities that were less densely populated were generally spared any interaction with cholera.

So where were all the doctors during these epidemics? Why did so many people die? Why didn't Americans have the necessary cures?

When people do not understand the cause of a disease, they look for someone or something to blame. In a sense, this man turning on a city water pipe was actually more to blame than people suspected at the time, since cholera was spread through public water supplies.

MISTAKING CAUSE FOR EFFECT.

Boy. "I SAY, TOMMY, I'M BLOW'D IF THERE ISN'T A MAN A TURNING ON THE CHOLERA."

The nineteenth century's new forms for transportation—including both riverboats and trains—meant that people could move more freely from place to place. Unfortunately, this also meant that they carried diseases from region to region.

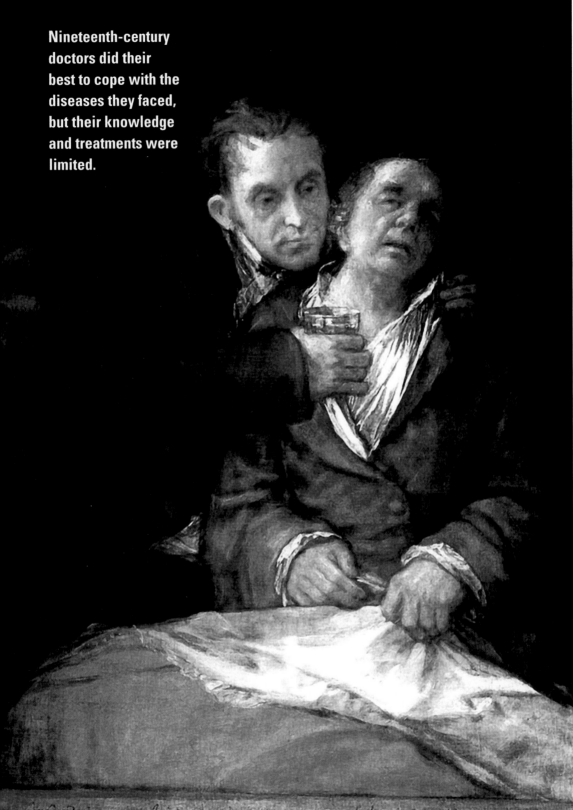

Nineteenth-century doctors did their best to cope with the diseases they faced, but their knowledge and treatments were limited.

Some doctors were available during these outbreaks. Many of them worked themselves to exhaustion trying to help the suffering. But they were essentially treading water in a sea of misinformation. Unlike today, when doctors diagnose a known disease and prescribe a scientifically tested cure, physicians of the nineteenth century were basing their treatments on ancient medical traditions. Some of these were helpful; many weren't. Some doctors had gone to school to study medicine, but the information taught at these school was also based on these same traditional practices. Many physicians in the 1800s had never gone to school; instead, they had been apprenticed for a period of a few years with an existing physician to gain the proper training. America had no system for the consistent accrediting of doctors, and different physicians often had very unique conceptual approaches to

This cartoon of a doctor staring into a beaker of water was meant to convey the extent of doctors' knowledge in the nineteenth century. Water gazing was a way of fortune telling, so the artist here is saying that the medical doctors of the 1800s were still using superstitions to try to heal people.

similar problems. Doctors rarely kept records of what treatments they had tried; they did not share what worked and didn't work with each other in medical journals, as is the practice in today's medical world.

Most ordinary people did not turn readily to a doctor for help if they fell ill. Instead, they relied on their own available resources before seeking outside assistance. Households had their own home remedies that were passed down through generations, and when those seemed as though they might fail, neighbors' remedies were attempted.

Folk medicine was alive and well in nineteenth-century America. The Native tribes had their own medical traditions, as did slave "root doctors," frontier grandmothers, and farmers who just thought they knew better than anyone else how to treat a variety of illnesses. In rural areas, people had all sorts of herbal mixtures they might concoct

Roots and plants like this—tansy—had been used for centuries to treat various ailments.

For centuries, women had taken care of women during and after childbirth.

from things in their garden or the surrounding woods.

When nineteenth-century women needed help during childbirth, they usually employed the services of a midwife rather than a physician. Throughout history, women known as midwives had always attended other women during childbirth, which was a dangerous time for both mothers and babies. Midwives had usually trained as apprentices under other midwives. Though their main purpose was to help during the delivery of babies, midwives in the early years of the 1800s were also healers in a more general sense.

EYEWITNESS ACCOUNT

Excerpts from the Diary of Midwife Martha Ballard, January 1801.

January 6, 1801
Snowed. John was very ill, Cony & Colman were called early this morn. Dressed the burns with poultices of rum, onions and Indian meal. Colman and Mrs Duttun with him this night. I laid down a little while in my clothes.

January 7, 1801
Snowed and hailed. Betsy came and helped do my work. John seems more comfortable. I was up the most of the night.

January 8, 1801
Snowed. John seems better. Mrs Woodward here to watch. I laid down in my clothes after mid night. Doctor Colman came after that and tarried the remainder of this night. I was called up at 5 to help dress John. He passed 1 worm.

January 9, 1801
Clear and cold. Colman went home. Cony came. John past 19 worms this day. His dad been twice to see him. Mr Ballard unwell. I feel so much fatigued, I can but just keep about.

January 10, 1801
Clear. I have had a fatiguing day. Jane Herington came at even to help me. Son Pollard called me at 9 to see his wife who is in labour.

January 11, 1801
Snowed and rained this morn. My Dear Daughter Pollard was at twelve-thirty this morn safe delivered of her second son & 5th child. I set up with her till 5. She was exhausted with pain & faintness, the infant seemed very unwell till then. Mrs Toll sett up all night. Daughter Lambdon came in the morn and I went on the bed and had the finest nap I have had since the first in this year. Mr Ballard came after me at 3 pm to come to Son Jonas wife who is in labour. She was safe delivered at 6.30 this even of her second daughter and 6th child. I tarried with her till 10 then came home and set with John till midnight.

In the 1800s, many people lived out of the reach of a practiced physician, on isolated farms or in tiny communities. Others simply didn't trust doctors, and some didn't want to pay for the services. And slaves often resisted help from their masters' white physicians, instead preferring to use their own healers and herbal medicines. The rich might call on physicians frequently, while still others would only use them if illness became serious. No matter how much money a person had, however, or where she went for medical care, the cures offered were more often than not insufficient. Many times, the patients would have actually been better off without the "help" of a physician.

Nonetheless, as the century pressed on, more and more men decided to become practicing physicians. Medicine was one of the fastest growing professions of the time. Young men went off to medical school, found apprenticeships, or simply taught and certified themselves. And yet little in the actual field of medicine was changing besides the number of doctors practicing.

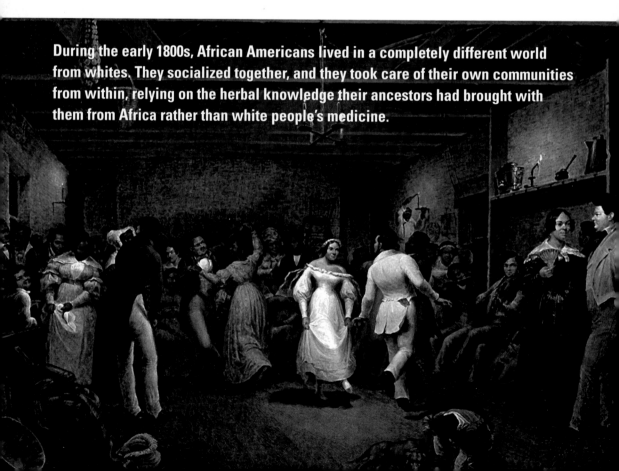

During the early 1800s, African Americans lived in a completely different world from whites. They socialized together, and they took care of their own communities from within, relying on the herbal knowledge their ancestors had brought with them from Africa rather than white people's medicine.

**Part II
New Perspectives
(1832–1865)**

1838

1838 Trail of Tears—General Winfield Scott and 7,000 troops force Cherokees to walk from Georgia to a reservation set up for them in Oklahoma (nearly 1,000 miles). Around 4,000 Native Americans die during the journey.

1839

1839 The first camera is patented by Louis Daguerre.

1844

1844 First public telegraph line in the world is opened—between Baltimore and Washington.

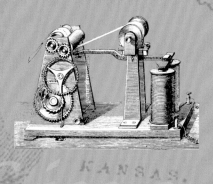

1853

1853 Yellow Fever kills some 7,849 people in New Orleans.

1854

1854 Kansas-Nebraska Act—States that each new state entering the country will decide for themselves whether or not to allow slavery. This goes directly against the terms agreed upon in the Missouri Compromise of 1820.

1859

1859 Louis Pasteur first suggests a "germ theory"—over the next ten years he develops the theory that tiny microorganisms spread diseases.

1846

1846 First painless surgery with a general anesthetic—William Morton, Boston dentist, designs a glass inhaler in which he places an ether-soaked sponge.

1847

1847 American Medical Association is founded.

1848

1848 Seneca Falls Convention—Feminist convention held for women's suffrage and equal legal rights.

1848(-58) California Gold Rush—Over 300,000 people flock to California in search of gold.

1849

1849 Elizabeth Blackwell is the first woman to receive a medical degree in the United States.

1861

1861(-65) Civil War —Fought between the Union and Confederate states.

1862

1862 Emancipation Proclamation—Lincoln states that all slaves in Union states are to be freed.

1865

1865 Thirteenth Amendment to the United States Constitution—Officially abolishes slavery across the country.

1865 President Abraham Lincoln is assassinated on April 15.

Imagine a doctor who shows up at your house and makes you sicker. It sounds ridiculous, but that's exactly what was happening all over the United States in the nineteenth century. You might think that having more doctors would have helped things, but when the knowledge those doctors are using is faulty, it doesn't matter how many professional physicians there are—people are still going to get sick and die. In many cases, in fact, the actions the doctors themselves took made their patients worse.

During the first part of the 1800s, most Americans still understood sickness the way it had been explained for thousands of years. Doctors believed that the human body contained four fluids or "humors"—blood, phlegm, bile, and black bile—and that when these humors were out of balance, illness occurred. Most medical treatments, in some way or another, focused on increasing or decreasing one or more of the four humors in an attempt to rebalance the system. Trained physicians of the time claimed that most illness was caused by "bodily excitement" that needed to be corrected. Their treatments almost always involved the draining of fluids from the body.

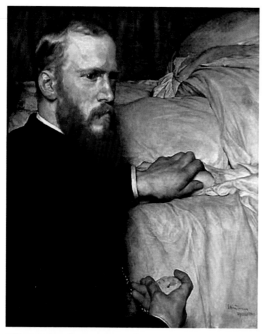

Nineteenth-century doctors meant well —but they often made a person even sicker than she had been to start with.

This old medical book (facing page) indicates the many places on the body where it was considered to be beneficial to drain blood or other fluids.

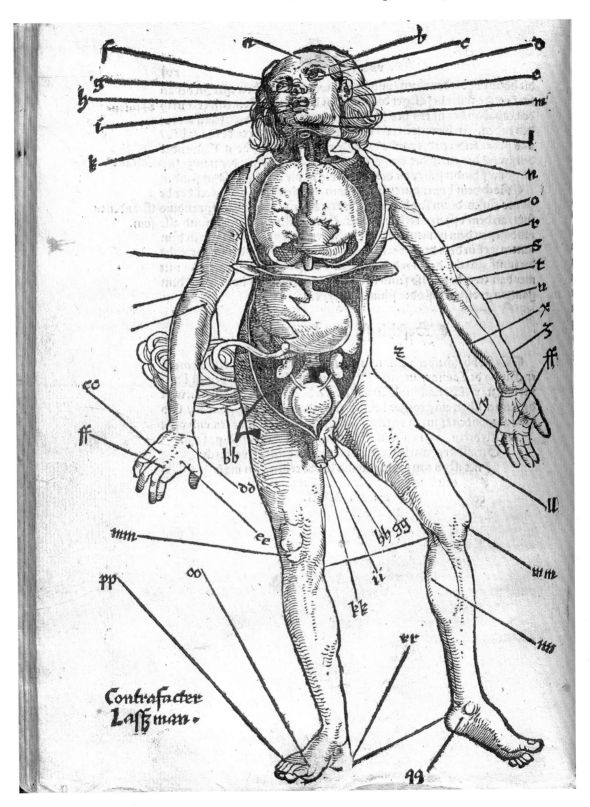

Contrafacter
Laßman.

In many ways, treatments were designed to create visible signs of change. Because people had such a limited understanding of the functioning of the human body, being able to see a physical change was reassuring to both the healers and patients. The most common remedies that American physicians and other healers of the times offered were bleeding, blistering, and purging (and sometimes vomiting), all of which brought about visible physical changes.

Imagine being wounded in a war—and then being "treated" by having more blood taken from you, followed by a medicine to make you throw up, followed at the end of all that by an enema to give you diarrhea!

Of these, bleeding was probably the most impressive. The practitioner would pierce one of the veins of the patient and allow blood to flow into a basin until he had judged that enough fluid had been taken. There was no set amount—they just eye-balled it. Some physicians went even farther and applied leeches directly to their patients' skin.

Blistering was used mostly for localized infections, injuries, or undefined pains. A caustic substance was first applied to the skin, raising large blisters. The blisters were then drained; doctors assumed the discharge removed the toxins causing the infection.

Even more frequently, however, doctors would try purging, which involved either administering powerful laxatives to induce diarrhea or taking large amounts of emetics (such as syrup of ipecac) to induce vomiting. Still other drugs induced salivation, sweating, and urination. The emission of fluids was the goal. Blood, sweat, vomit, and pus—these were the tangible evidence that the treatment was "working."

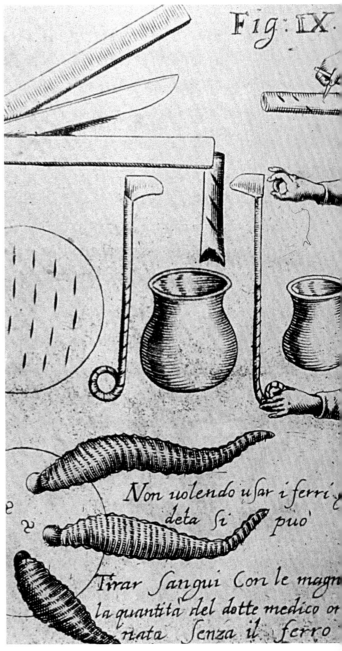

The instruments—and creatures—doctors used during bloodletting are shown here.

By the mid 1830s, though, skepticism about such practices was growing among certain physicians, and some began to practice "physiobotanic" medicine. They claimed these plant-based remedies were far safer than the orthodox techniques of bleeding or offering harsher drugs. Meanwhile, "homeopathic" doctors tended to prescribe the classic drugs but in a much diluted state. Even so, these alternate approaches didn't really offer much variation of the standard treatments. Homeopathic doctors were giving the same medicine, just less of it, and botanical doctors were often offering remedies that, although plant-based, caused the same results (like vomiting).

So did any of these treatments help at all? Not really. While some of the herbal remedies may have aided the body's natural defenses, they mostly helped to relieve symptoms. In a few cases, lowering a patient's blood pressure might have been worthwhile to help the patient's muscles relax, but bloodletting more often than not severely weakened the patient at a time when he was in the most need of his strength. Imagine being deathly sick—and then having a

Samuel Hahnemann was the father of homeopathy. He believed that a medical practitioner had only three options: first, what he called "sublime," was to remove the cause of disease, something that could seldom occur in the 1800s; second, the treatment by opposites, such as laxatives for constipation, which he called "palliative;" and third, the method he recommended, treatment by similars, in which like cures like. In other words, a doctor would prescribe a little bit of the very thing that caused the same symptom the patient was experiencing, in an effort to stimulate the body's natural defense responses. Homeopathic practitioners still exist in the twenty-first century.

If nothing else, doctors provided a sympathetic ear to upper-class nineteenth-century women.

doctor cut your skin to make you bleed. If you weren't going to die to start with, you might very well do so from blood loss! Or think about the last time you had the flu—and then imagine that a doctor showed up to make you violently throw up—or gave you blisters along with your other already unpleasant symptoms!

But medical advancements did take place. The fact that people were trying different medicines and considering different perspectives was a positive first step. This outside-the-box thinking is what led Crawford W. Long to perform the first successful surgery using ether as an anesthetic. On March 30, 1842, he painlessly removed a tumor from the neck of a patient. Other advances came later in the century, during the unfortunate, violent dispute between the American North and South—the Civil War.

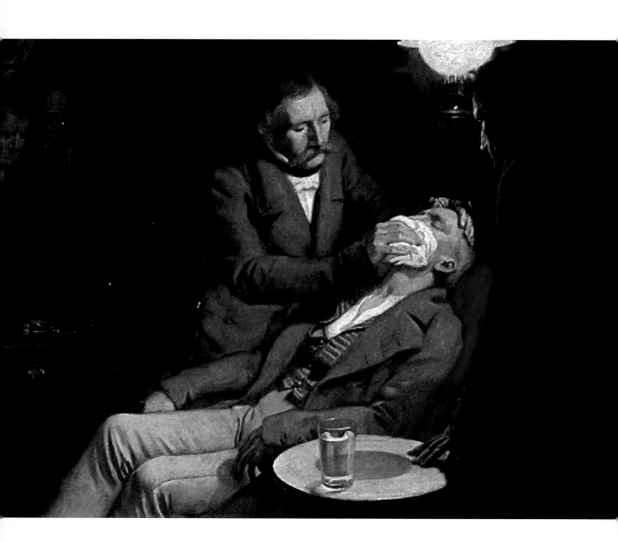

INCREDIBLE INDIVIDUAL
Crawford W. Long

Crawford Long was born in Danielsville, Georgia, on March 1, 1815. He attended medical school at the University of Pennsylvania, receiving his medical degree in 1839. He then studied surgery in New York until moving back to Georgia and setting up a practice in Jefferson in 1841. On March 30, 1842, Long performed the first successful surgery using ether as an anesthetic, removing a tumor from the neck of James M. Venable. After this success, Long used ether in this manner whenever possible, but he did not publish his findings until 1849. By then though, in Boston in 1846, William Morton had publicly demonstrated the use of ether, and as a result, Long's recognition was lessened. Today, however, he is properly remembered as the one who initiated ether's surgical use.

In 1851 he moved to Athens, Georgia, and set up a new practice that thrived. He lived there the rest of his life, until he died in July of 1878.

Using ether as an anesthetic allowed doctors to perform painless surgeries; dentists could also pull teeth while their patients were unconscious. Unfortunately, when the patient woke up, he would still have to cope with the pain!

Initially during the Civil War, neither side employed very many doctors. No one expected the conflict to last as long as it did or to be as bloody as it was. The combination of rifled guns, deadly ball ammunition, and close-quarters, old-war tactics, however, led to an immense number of dead and wounded. As the war continued, more and more doctors had to be recruited. But very few of these doctors were skilled in the one area of medicine that would become all too common during the war—surgery.

But they would get experience. If you were a doctor during the Civil War, you had no choice. No matter what kind of medicine you had practiced before the war, you would need to develop surgical skills now to meet the demands of wartime. The most common form of surgery was amputation. Soldiers that were shot in the head or chest were often left to die, as it was considered almost impossible to help them.

Unfortunately, Civil War surgeries were often more deadly than the battlefields themselves. You might think it was obvious that before you cut into someone, you should clean your instruments and wash your hands. But this was not obvious to doctors

A train of ambulances waits to carry the wounded from the battlefield to the doctors who will do their best to treat their wounds.

The wounded wait to be treated at a Civil War hospital in Fredericksburg, Virginia.

during the mid-1800s. Surgeons often performed surgery after surgery without ever washing, using the same bloody sponges, cloths, and tools. Many patients were treated right on the ground, with no concern for the dirt and other conditions of the battlefield. Tools were primitive; a basic surgeon's kit included a saw, pliers, hooks, and a few knives of varying sizes. Since antibiotics hadn't been discovered yet, infection was rampant.

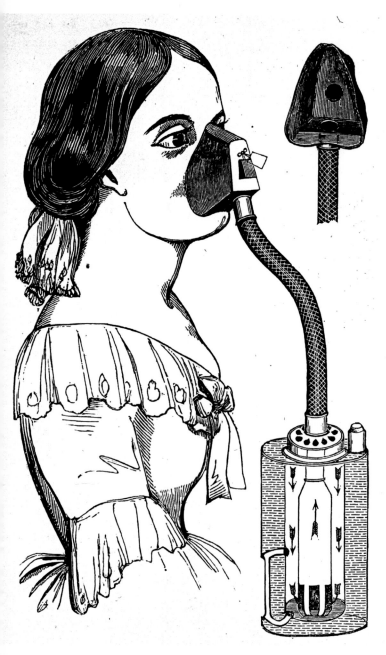

The one tool doctors did have that at least helped the patient endure the pain was chloroform. This was used to put patients to sleep, so it kept them from feeling pain during the operation.

As bad as the Civil War was, it did have one benefit: doctors learned and began to change their practices as a result of their experiences during the war. By the end of the war, surgeons were performing amputations much more efficiently, in around ten minutes, and the government developed the Sanitary Commission, which made great strides toward educating people on how and why to keep hospitals and camps more sanitary. These were the first steps toward a healthier future.

Like ether, chloroform meant that a patient could be made unconscious during surgery. It was administered via a contraption that looked like this.

Part III
After the War
(1865–1900)

1867

1867 United States purchases Alaska from Russia.

1867 John Lister publishes the Antiseptic Principle of the Practice of Surgery—leads to cleaning surgical instruments and wounds, helps decrease deaths from infection.

1869

1869 Transcontinental Railroad completed on May 10.

1870

1870 Fifteenth Amendment to the United States Constitution— Prohibits any citizen from being denied to vote based on their "race, color, or previous condition of servitude."

1870 Christmas is declared a national holiday.

1882

1882 Louis Pasteur develops a rabies vaccine.

1886

1886 The Statue of Liberty is dedicated on October 28.

1890

1890 Wounded Knee Massacre— Last battle in the American Indian Wars.

1890 Emil von Behring discovers antitoxins— leads to tetanus and diphtheria vaccines.

1892

1892 Ellis Island is opened to receive immigrants coming into New York.

1876

1876 Alexander Graham Bell invents the telephone.

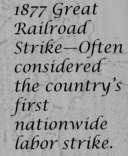

1877

1877 Great Railroad Strike—Often considered the country's first nationwide labor strike.

1878

1878 Thomas Edison patents the phonograph on February 19.

1878 Thomas Edison invents the light bulb on October 22.

1879

1879 First vaccine for cholera.

of the 1800s

1895

1895 Wilhelm Conrad Röntgen discovers X-rays for medical imaging.

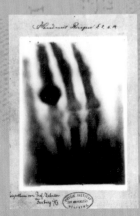

1896

1896 Plessy vs. Ferguson—Supreme Court case that rules that racial segregation is legal as long as accommodations are kept equal.

1896 Henry Ford builds his first combustion-powered vehicle, which he names the Ford Quadricycle.

1898

1898 The Spanish-American War—The United States gains control of Cuba, Puerto Rico, and the Philippines.

After the Civil War, Americans tried to get back to normal life. They picked up their work on farms, and in shops. Former African American slaves, as well as many whites, ventured out into the unknown territory of freedom. Those moving westward dealt with interactions with Native tribes who were being pushed into a shrinking territory.

During the 1800s, country doctors made their rounds with horse and buggies. When a family member was sick or a woman was in labor, an urgent plea often went out to the doctor.

Childbirth was a dangerous time during the 1800s, both for the mother and for her child.

Everyone got back to the business of marrying, having babies, and raising families.

That process was an important part of the reconstruction of the American identity, as a new generation was raised in a unified country. That next generation did not enter the world alone. Their mothers and fathers welcomed them . . . and so did doctors and midwives.

Snapshot from the Past
The Sounds of Birth

John could hear the screaming all night long. He didn't sleep. His mother was only one room over, the walls in their small farmhouse were thin, and things were just too loud.

John had been looking forward to holding his new brother or sister. The year before, when John was twelve, his mother had given birth to a daughter, but the baby came down with an awful fever in her first month and was dead in a few days. John had helped his parents name her—Annabella. The year before that, his mother had also had a baby girl, but something had gone wrong while she was being born, and she had never even cried. They had named that baby Alice.

The midwife had arrived the day before, and she had not left his mother's side since. At first John had been allowed to go in and out of his parents' room freely, talking to his mother when he wanted, but now the door was shut, and when John knocked he was told to go away. He was worried. He didn't want to have another dead sister to name.

But he was even more worried when the screaming stopped.

He had lost track of time, lying in his bed wondering what it would be like to have a little brother or sister, and he hadn't noticed the lull at first. When he did, he sat up. Listened.

Silence.

John heard his own pulse thudding in his ears.

And then he heard something, a faint cry. But it was not his mother. It was too small a noise.

John smiled. He couldn't tell yet if the cry came from the mouth of a girl or a boy, but he was sure there was a baby in the house. Then he heard his mother's voice, sounding both joyful and tired, and he knew that all was well.

All he could do now was pray that the baby stayed healthy.

Children's Health

Birth was a dangerous event, both for mothers and babies, and even in the second half of the nineteenth century, that had not yet changed. Even if a baby managed to be safely born, her life was fragile, and in the first year of her life, she was especially at risk.

Before antibiotics and immunizations became available in the twentieth century, infectious disease was the biggest killer. One white baby out of every six or seven did not make it past their first birthday. And for the babies of black Americans, the survival rate was even lower. Children who made it through infancy were still at risk; they often died from diphtheria, whooping cough, and scarlet fever. The ordinary viral infections of childhood, like measles, mumps, and chicken pox, frequently led to deadly secondary infections. Between the ages of one and twenty-one years of age, another 8 to 10 percent of children died, meaning that one out of every four or five children would not live to adulthood. These numbers are staggering to our modern ears, since nowadays birth is often seen as routine, and childhood is considered the safest period of a person's life.

Children could be happy and playing one day—and be deathly sick the next. In a world with no antibiotics or vaccinations, even ordinary illnesses could turn deadly.

Imagine being a child in a time
when the odds were good that
you wouldn't live to grow up!

Dental Health

Dental care was another major issue in the nineteenth century. Today, most of us are taught from a young age to brush and take care of our teeth, and as a result, many people face few if any major issues with their teeth for the entirety of their lives. In the 1800s, that was very different. Although tooth brushes were available fairly early in the century, they were seen as a novelty rather than a necessity; people didn't brush or pay attention to dental care. Having a tooth pulled was an all-too-common procedure. Early in the century, before anesthetics were available, this would have been extremely painful. Yet it was also one of the few medical procedures that could be expected to go well (barring infection). If you had a toothache, you could usually count on feeling much better once the tooth was pulled.

The irony surrounding this common problem was that the tooth loss and gum disease were sometimes caused by mercury in the medicines and remedies people took for other ailments.

If you think going to the dentist is bad now, imagine what it was like in the nineteenth century!

A nineteenth-century ad for toothbrushes. Notice how much longer the brushes were than the ones we're used to today.

Pharmaceutical Medicine

During the Civil War, a new profession arose: pharmacists who mixed and dispensed medicine. After the war, pharmacists began to open drug stores. Now when people got sick, they had another place to turn: they could go to the drugstore and buy medicine.

Back in the 1800s, you didn't need a doctor's prescription for any kind of medicine, and at first, pharmacists made every drug they dispensed from scratch. As the century wore on, however, drug manufacturers began to get rich mass producing medicine. These drugs were referred to as patent medicines.

Each drug manufacturer had its own formulas, and marketed their medicines under a variety of names. Mail-order companies like Sears and Wards had large sections of their catalogs devoted to patent medicines. One of these remedies was called "Sooth-

By the end of the 1800s, at least one patent medicine almanac like this one was printed for every two Americans. Their primary purpose was to sell their products. The covers featured attractive subjects such as idealized rural scenes, rosy-cheeked children, and pretty young women. Others sought to impress with a picture of an imposing manufacturing building, or suggested a link between their product and the natural medical practices of the Indians.

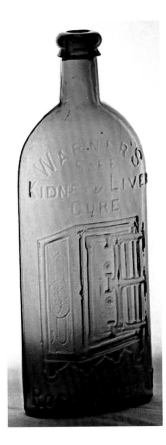

ing Baby Syrup." It claimed to calm fussy babies and put them to sleep. Since its primary ingredient was opium, it really worked! Unfortunately, many babies ended up as opium addicts. Other drugs contained alcohol and cocaine. Some didn't contain much of anything at all.

Not all patent medicines were dangerous or fake. Pharmacists experimented with combinations of drugs that seemed most effective, and some of them worked. Drugs like albuteral, quinine, digoxin, aspirin, and morphine, still in use today, began to be used in the late 1800s. In the nineteenth century, however, the government did not regulate these drugs in any way. They could be made by anyone and dispensed to anyone.

Medicine bottles like these were a common sight in most nineteenth-century homes. You didn't need a doctor's prescription—and you didn't REALLY know what you were taking. People could decide for themselves what medicines they needed. This meant that an individual might be taking lots of medicines, some of them helpful, some of them dangerous, and some that did nothing, all for the same condition.

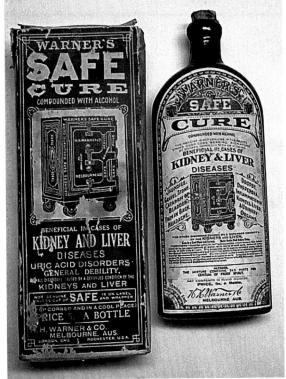

Native Medicines

Although nineteenth-century pharmacists often tried out Native remedies in their medicines, the doctors of the day looked down on the medicine practiced outside the European tradition. In the 1800s, as today, non-Western perspectives on medicine were quite different.

Traditional Native medicine varied from group to group. Most tribes used various plant-based remedies to treat disease and other health problems. In addition, in many tribes, illness was believed to have a spiritual element as well, which meant a sick person could only find a cure via spiritual intervention. Medicine men (or women), called shamans in some groups, could communicate with the spirit world and act as healers. Today, modern medicine affirms the perspective that disease has both emotional and physical elements, but nineteenth-century doctors scoffed at these traditional medicines as being inferior to the "modern medicine" of the day.

Native people saw spirit and body as linked together, rather than two separate pieces of a human being as Western medicine has often done.

EYEWITNESS ACCOUNT

(From an article for the Transactions of the American Medical Association, Vol. 15, 1864)

The State of medical knowledge among these Indians (Onondagas) may be briefly told. Their knowledge of remedies and of diseases is so vague and limited that it is a marvel why any sane quack should think to add to his popularity by styling himself an Indian Doctor, or should hope to increase the sale of his nostrums, by giving them the Christian name of some unpronounceable Indian tribe. A few roots, leaves, and barks of recognized medicinal powers, such as black cohosh, mandrake, apocynum, and spigelia, and many more of no potency for good or evil, as witch-hazel, wild grape-vine roots, angelica, fire-weed, together with Epsom salts and castor oil, make up the most of their Materia Medica. They have here a chief who glories also in the title of Indian Doctor, who practices a little in the tribe, and among some of the ignorant and credulous whites in the surrounding section. He is very limited in his remedies, but makes up the lack in boasts and pretensions. . . .

There are a few squaws who dispense mysteriously manipulated compounds of roots, leaves, and barks, infused in large quantities of warm water, given warm, or added to rum or whiskey, and given for months to chronic invalids; but none of these ever extract teeth, bleed, cup, adjust broken or dislocated bones, or open swellings—for all surgery or operative midwifery they depend on "white doctors" or nature, and so destitute were they of the means of paying for medical and surgical attendance, even where they might have disposition to pay, that nature had been trusted to in many cases where timely aid might have saved life, or preserved limbs from terrible distortion.

Although the medical community scoffed at Native medicine, ordinary people often respected Native knowledge—and pharmaceutical companies took advantage of this by claiming that their products were based on Native remedies (though they seldom were).

Traveling salesmen went from town to town selling their medical remedies. These were often flamboyant show-men who provided entertainment as much or more than they did actual medical treatments.

Despite the medical community's negative viewpoint, many traditional Native medicines (or medicines sold as such) were very popular among the general public. Many of these patent medicines were made up by individuals looking to get rich quickly. These "snake-oil" salesmen used the reputation of Indian cures to pedal what were usually ineffective concoctions. Instead of being based in real Native tradition, they were simply mixtures that contained high concentrations of alcohol, cocaine, or heroin.

A Different Time

We live in a time of cushioned beds, proper balanced diets, over-the-counter pain medicines like aspirin and acetaminophen, and well-trained doctors and dentists. Many people work physically easier jobs where they spend most of the day sitting. Children are protected from diseases by immunizations. Our government makes sure that new drugs are carefully tested before being released to the public, and it keeps track of infectious diseases in an attempt to avoid dangerous outbreaks. If we're bleeding, we know to stop it. If we're sick, we know to avoid activities that would weaken us. We at least somewhat understand why we get sick and how germs are passed from person to person.

People in the nineteenth century didn't have these advantages. They lived lives that were physically challenging, but they pushed through pain that would have incapacitated modern Americans, working full days on the farm with dislocated joints and badly-set broken bones. Often people lived with uncomfortable and painful skin irritations and illnesses for years, considering themselves essentially healthy.

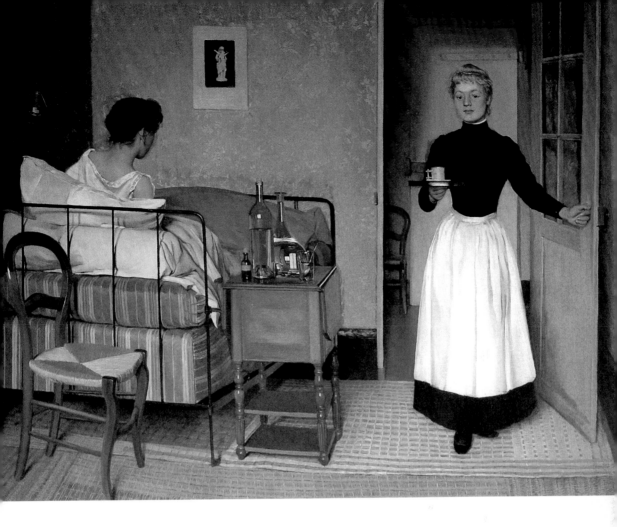

And people died young a lot more often than they do today. Today, we think of death as something unusual and tragic, especially when it strikes a younger person. Most of us live longer, healthier lives, and childhood deaths are rare. But just 200 years ago, parents were braced for their children's deaths, knowing that if they gave birth to five children, odds were good they would lose at least one. Some parents had no children survive. During the 1800s, no one was untouched by death. Marriages weren't broken up by divorce as they are today, but instead, death split people's unions. In other cases, both parents might fall ill and die, leaving behind orphans who would be sent off to live with relatives or be adopted by neighbors.

In many ways, the inability to overcome health issues shaped the reality people experienced during the nineteenth century. Today, many of our most common causes of death are (at least to some extent) self-inflicted. Because we drive everywhere, deaths from car accidents happen in large numbers—but this risk did not exist in nineteenth-century America. Because people now have unhealthy diets and sedentary lifestyles, obesity and heart disease are common—but people who ate less and did physical labor all day long were far less likely to develop these diseases. We have made progress in some areas, but at the same time, we have also encountered new problems.

In a time when most people were farmers—or did hard manual labor in factories—few people were obese.

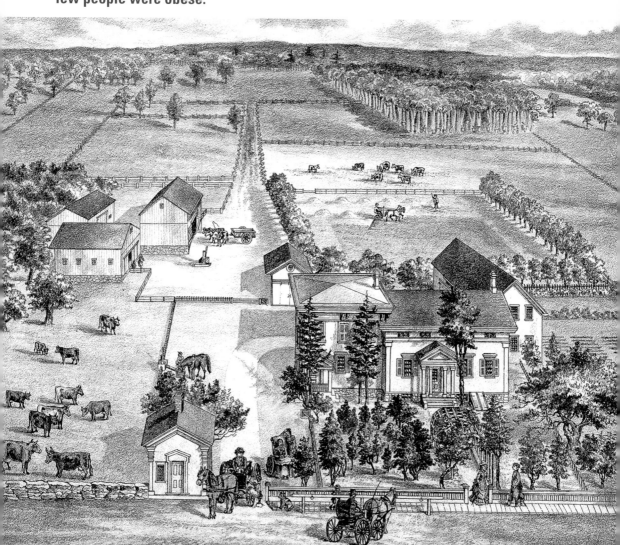

EXTRA! EXTRA!

National Anti-Slavery Standard
New York, Saturday 24
July 1869

Dr. Elizabeth Blackwell, twenty-five years ago, was denied admission to all the medical schools of New York, Philadelphia and Boston; but her great perseverance at last opened for her the doors of Geneva College, from which starting-point she has gone steadily onward to her present honored and influential position. But it is needless to multiply examples. Their name is legion. Furthermore, there is a change going on in public opinion which will ultimately make the education of girls of paramount importance in the estimation of all classes. God speed the day of this awakening. Vassar College is one of the signs of its coming; and another is the universal agitation of the question: "Shall women learn the alphabet?" with all its correlatives and consequences. Thirty-four graduates went forth from Vassar College at this year's close, and they, with the Alumni of past and future years, will represent a higher type of womanhood. Let

woman be truly educated, and we may confidently prophesy a higher type of humanity, since she is the Mother of the Race.

Looking back at medicine in the 1800s, we may feel as though doctors and their patients at the very least lacked common sense—and that at worst, doctors and pharmacists may have taken advantage of people's illnesses and gullibility. But people in the 1800s were not dumb, and most doctors and pharmacists were not evil. Remember, hindsight is twenty-twenty! Nineteenth-century physicians thought they were practicing the pinnacle of modern medicine. They would also have looked back at past generations and marveled at how far medicine had come, just as we do today. What are we doing today that future generations will look back at and marvel at for being stupid and nonsensical?

The important thing is that Americans in the 1800s were not defeated by the medical challenges they faced. People didn't abandon their cities from the fear of unstoppable epidemics. Civil War doctors didn't give up in the face of wave after wave of dying soldiers. They learned from and gradually overcame the challenges they faced. We will need the same drive today as we face new health issues that challenge even the best medical minds of today.

The doctors of the nineteenth century laid the groundwork for today's medical system.

Think About It

In the 1800s, many babies, children, and young people died from diseases and infections that are easily controlled today, and epidemic diseases killed thousands. New drugs and improved medical treatments in the late 1800s lengthened the lifespan of the average American by more than ten years, but early death was still much more common than it is today.

- How do you think the frequency of babies and small children dying affected parents in the 1800s? How might it have influenced their religious beliefs, the way they viewed pregnancy, and their relationships with their children?

- How do you think living with the possibility of dying young might change the way you look at life?

- What would it be like to live in a city where thousands of people were dying of a disease that had no known cause and absolutely no hope for a cure?

- How do you think a modern city would deal with an epidemic disease on the scale of the Asiatic cholera epidemic in 1832?

Words Used in This Book

accrediting: Giving official approval that someone's professional abilities meet an acceptable standard.

apprentices: People training for a job under the direction of someone already established in the business or profession.

botanical: Substances derived from plants.

emission: The passing of a fluid out of the body.

epidemic: A disease that is quickly spreading through a community and affecting large numbers of people.

ether: A colorless and odorless liquid that, when the fumes are breathed in, causes unconsciousness; used as an anesthetic.

intemperance: Bad habits, especially the abuse of alcohol.

paramount: Of great importance.

pinnacle: At the very top, most advanced level.

potency: The strength of a medicine, usually measured by its concentration.

rampant: Uncontrolled energy and growth.

skepticism: A questioning attitude and approach to facts and ideas.

validated: Something that has been proven to be true.

Find Out More

In Books

Bethard, Wayne. *Lotions, Potions, and Deadly Elixirs: Frontier Medicine in America.* Latham, Md.: Roberts Rinehart, 2004.

Rutkow, Ira. *Seeking the Cure: A History of Medicine in America.* New York: Simon & Schuster, 2010.

Schroeder-Lein, Glenna R. *The Encyclopedia of Civil War Medicine.* Armonk, N.Y.: B. E Sharpe, 2008.

On the Internet

Cholera in 1832
www.virtualny.cuny.edu/cholera/1832/cholera_1832_set.html

Maggots and leeches
www.livescience.com/health/050419_maggots.html

Pain and cleanliness
www.sciencemuseum.org.uk/broughttolife/themes/surgery/pain.aspx

Patent medicines
www.drugstoremuseum.com/sections/level_info2.php?level=3&level_id=26

Index

Picture Credits

About the Author and the Consultant

Matthew Ronald Strange is a writer living in Richmond, Virginia. He has worked as an editor and as a copywriter, but his true passion is writing creatively: short stories, poetry, and maybe someday a novel. This is his first time writing for Mason Crest.

John Gillis is a Rutgers University Professor of History Emeritus. A graduate of Amherst College and Stanford University, he has taught at Stanford, Princeton, University of California at Berkeley, as well as Rutgers. Gillis is well known for his work in social history, including pioneering studies of age relations, marriage, and family. The author or editor of ten books, he has also been a fellow at both St. Antony's College, Oxford, and Clare Hall, Cambridge.

—